Make a Finger Puppet

Dee White
Photography by Alice McBroom

You can make a finger puppet.

You will need:

a drawing of a prince

a drawing of a princess

Colour in the dragon.

Cut it out. Cut two holes for your fingers.

Put two fingers in the holes.

Now your dragon can walk.

Colour in the prince and princess.

Cut them out. Cut the holes for your fingers.

Put two fingers in the holes.

Now your prince and princess can run.

Play with your puppets. Have fun!